ABSENTEE INDIANS

Native American Series
Clifford Trafzer, *series editor*

To Be the Main Leaders of Our People:
A History of Minnesota Ojibwe Politics, 1825–1898
Rebecca Kugel

Indian Summers
Eric Gansworth

The Feathered Heart
Mark Turcotte

Tortured Skins
Maurice Kenny

Nickel Eclipse: Iroquois Moon
Eric Gansworth

In the Time of the Present
Maurice Kenny

"We Are Not Savages":
Native Americans in Southern California and the
Pala Reservation, 1840–1920
Joel R. Hyer

Combing the Snakes from His Hair
James Thomas Stephens

Absentee Indians and Other Poems
Kimberly Blaeser

ABSENTEE INDIANS

& *Other Poems*

Kimberly Blaeser

Michigan State University Press
East Lansing

Michigan State University Press
East Lansing, Michigan 48823–5254

Printed and bound in the United States of America.

07 06 05 04 03 02 01   1 2 3 4 5 6 7 8 9 10

LIBRARY OF CONGRESS CATALOGING-IN-PUBLICATION DATA

Blaeser, Kimberly M.
Absentee Indians and other poems / by Kimberly Blaeser.
  p. cm. — (Native American series)
ISBN 0-87013-607-0 (pbk.: alk. paper)
  1. Indians of North America—Poetry. I. Title. II. Series.
PS3552.L3438 A625 2002
811'.54—DC21

                                        2002006987

Cover artwork by David Bradley
Book cover and interior design by Valerie Brewster,
Scribe Typography

Visit Michigan State University Press
on the World Wide Web at:
www.msupress.msu.edu

for Gavin and Amber Dawn

Contents

Acknowledgements

In the writing of these poems support came in various forms from my family and friends. I particularly want to thank members of the Word Warriors writers' network, especially Amy DeJarlais, Lupe Solis, Chris Fink, Peter Whalen, Steve Kirk, Kyoko Yoshida, Michael McDaniel, Michael Roberts, Karen Howland, Jill Zellmer, Kirsten Hemmy, and Theresa Delgadillo. I am grateful for the support of Wordcraft Circle and the Native Writers' Circle of the Americas and to many individuals within these organizations, especially Gordon Henry, Denise Sweet, Lee Francis, Joe and Carol Bruchac, and Gerald Vizenor. My thanks to John Crawford who offered comments on the manuscript and to Antone Treur, teacher and tutor of the Ojibwe language. I offer sincere thanks to the editors and program planners who have offered me chances to share my work. And I thank my family — nuclear, extended, and by affection — who nurtured me during these years of change and helped me carve out time for my writing. Thank you to Pam Swanson, Amanda Bloss, and Jill Rehberg for childcare and to Leonard Wardzala for endless care.

Grateful acknowledgement is made to the editors of the following publications in which some of these poems first appeared: *The Cimarron Review*, "Absentee Indians;" *Luna: A New Journal of Poetry and Translation*, "Recite the Names of All the Suicided Indians," and "lament;" *Gatherings: The En'owkin Journal of First North American Peoples, Vol. VIII; Shaking the Belly, Releasing the Sacred Clown*, "Students of Scat," "Are you sure Hank done it this way?" and "Don't Burst the Bubble;" *Free Lunch*, "Twelve Steps to Ward Off Homesickness;" *Native American Songs and Poems*, "Anza Borrego, 1995;" *The Cream City Review*, "your old lost loves;" *Steam Ticket, A Third Coast Review*, "Imprints in Blackfeet Country," and "Cerca de Aquí;" *Saint Paul Pioneer Press*, "In the Tradition of the Peacemakers;" *Dreaming History: A Collection of Wisconsin Native American Writing*, "Meeting Place," and "Those Things That

Come to You at Night;" *Wildfire; Volume One: Inner Weavings*, "Night Tremors;" *Wisconsin Academy Review,* "Y2K Indian;" *My Home as I Remember,* "Kitchen Voices;" *Rampike,* "This Guy Back Home" and "letter, from one half mad writer to another;" and *South Dakota Review,* "The Last Fish House."

Note on the spelling of Ojibwe words: All words are spelled using the double vowel system with two exceptions: When using the name of a town or village for which a different and standard spelling is generally in use, I employ that popular spelling. When words are meant to allude to another literary work, the spelling employed in that original work is used here as well.

Preface

Another absentee Indian dreams of home. Places and seasons drift timeless, faces fluid and ageless. Tastes these migrations like ripe plums filled with soft pulp, sun warm, sweet. Like round vowels of midnight stories, overheard and sorted in the mists of a small girl's memory. Sorted with the unending litters of fat new puppies once birthed and mothered beneath the porch on Grandpa Antell's farm. Imagines the nests of musty hay and each dram of full warm earth breath. Now craving the mouths of puppies, the musk of childhood.

Another absentee Indian, home to visit. Pines grow tall in my absence, cousins grow up, parents grow old. Houses of child memory contract, fold in on themselves, tumble down into rubble. And still the years bind us, our souls held in a hot prison of longing. Like the bumblebees of childhood whisked off the nectar of hollyhocks, captured in a mason jar, breathing through so many knife cuts. Two long weekends each year. Thanksgiving, Christmas, maybe Easter. A dying mother, an aging father. Connections rust like abandoned cars. Remembrances piled behind family homes, rifled for parts.

Another absentee Indian brings home a child. Stands this ground, the place of history. Claiming home, asks a blessing. Picks up the snatches of language. Repeats them. Practices survival like she is learning the recipes for baking powder biscuits, venison sausage, or dill pickles. Measures by memory the distances to each rice bed, sugar camp, burial ground. The distance to the seventh generation. Names the markers, like she was writing a pathway.

ABSENTEE INDIANS

Absentee Indians

Used to think they were white.
They'd come
visiting Grandma's.
Big cars,
neat little
quiet
scrubbed-looking kids
in matching tennies.
Come from somewheres else for sure.
Sundays
or maybe just seeming like it,
and acting like a holiday too.
Absentee Indians.
Back for a memory
a fix if they could find it
get them through
till next pow-wow
sugarbush
funeral
next lonely.
Old Man Blues we call it,
emptiness bubbling up like a blister
ready to pop.
Ain't no cure for it
but home.

Now it's me returning
going visiting
making the rez rounds
like all the other absentee Indians.
A week to see my whole family.

Twenty-five minutes apiece each.
Picnic at Coffee Pot landing
fishing at Uddies
berry picking, sausage making,
one of every good thing squeezed in.
Hardly time enough
this trip
but making plans
next trip.
Litanies of family names,
river talk, hollows,
reciting hunting camps,
pine-pitch memories
what used to be.
Hoarding remainders
things never meant to be counted
like prayer breaths.
Searching some magic antidote
boiling pine boughs
some sequence of recall
twelve steps
to ward off homesickness.

"Twice a year I come
to see the folks," he said.
A city Indian
some relative from California.
"Summers I bring the kids.
Want them to learn about their heritage."
We used to laugh
when he said heritage
like every book on Indians
instead of people or tribe or life.

Ain't hardly laughing now.

Twelve Steps to Ward Off Homesickness

I

Eat oatmeal and bacon for breakfast. Fry eggs in bacon grease and eat over cold oatmeal for lunch. Make macaroni and canned tomatoes for supper. Repeat for 5 days.

II

Scatter machine parts around your lawn. Volunteer to let a friend set his old beater up on blocks in your yard.

III

Check four dogs out of the pound for the weekend. Let them all run loose. Then try to jog or take long walks.

IV

Look in the mirror and say "Damn Indian" until you get it right. Stop only when you remember the voice of every law officer that ever chanted those words.

V

Light cigarettes and place them in ashtrays throughout your house. Inhale.

VI

Enter your car through the passenger door. Drive it without using reverse. Continue for one week or until you remember a rez car is not a picturesque metaphor.

VII

Read the police report in your hometown paper. Read the letters to the editor in your tribal paper. Read the minutes from the last RBC meeting. Read the propaganda from each candidate in the tribal election. List every area of disagreement and try to decide who is telling the truth.

VIII

In summer, turn off the AC and open the windows to let in the flies and mosquitos.

IX

Take your morning vitamin with warm, flat beer — 3.2 if you can get it. Follow with yesterday's coffee heated over. Repeat daily until the urge to drive across three states disappears.

X

Call home to find out how all the relatives are getting along.

XI

Recite the names of all the suicided Indians.

XII

If all else fails, move back.

Recite the Names of All the Suicided Indians

I

Do it under your breath he said,
this guy back home.
Telling me something
about chanting.
Until the little bones
behind each ear
pound.
And the air swirls
off the sides
of your tongue.
Until the words
become
small projectiles.
Huffed out
of your chest
alive.

II

His uncle's boy
handcuffed
roughed up.
Hard set chin
quivering
beneath cakes of blood.
His little sister
crooked braid

falling down her back
falling down
hung over
from her first big drunk.
Those times
he stood by.
Without the words.

III

Whittling matchsticks
drumming
humming with his fingertips.
Lighting smoking-wicked lamps
that smell like stories.
Shuffling decks of cards
and playing them out
hand
after aging
hand.
Betting on memories
we gather here
in his house,
Until someone's ghost
begins to sing
and this year
finally
we learn to join in.

IV

Obituaries
read like tribal rolls
he says,

and saves his rice money.
Memorial wreathes
cost more each year.
Too many die
from lack of the language.
Too many too young
too Indian or too little.

Gashkendam.
He is lonesome.
So many gone silent
like the songs.
Go deaf if you must he said
but keep singing your name
your life
keep singing
your name
your life.
Nagamon.
Sing.

        v

So let me
chant
for you
each one
the names
of all
the suicided
Indians.

This Guy Back Home

Always the last fish house
left on the lake.
Day he pulls it out
the ice breaks up.
He's that kind.
The one all the old ladies want
to take to bingo
and not just for his luck.
He's the kind
can make everyone laugh
can sing Indian songs
can wear his hair long
swaying
as he shadow boxes
the county sheriff.
Watch that one...
my uncle says,
and I say *Yesss.*

The Last Fish House

January crosses the calendar
like a good story.
Slow and steaming breath
words swirling
up our ankles.
Wind drifts shapes
we tell and can taste
like meringue tufts of memory.
Derbies, fish shacks, poker runs.
Winter ages slowly.

Now metal runners squeak across frozen lake.
Hand-fashioned wooden sled
heavy with spears, decoys, auger and ice-fishing rigs.
Single-handed he clasps the thick, frayed rope,
pulling the collection of candles, stringers and pails,
thermos, sandwiches, pickles, and fish house candy.
Behind, silver minnow bucket sloshes
its cutting weight passed
from gloved hand to gloved hand
as we follow him follow the tire tracks
avoid each open angling hole
leave the tree-lined shore
squint tearing into rays
sharpened light on white on ice.
Oversized boots insulate
toes wiggle giddy with excitement.
"Which one is ours?"
"Who's going to spear first?"
"Are we going to use Les Hanson's house, too?"

Stand now in the moment of arrival
each breathless with the efforts
of journey,   of quiet centering
in the blue white middle of being
here.
Thick-parka-clad and bright-colored
flashes upon the revolutions of ice
encircled by barren arbor
womb-covered by winter sky.
Here.
In the turning compass of time
in the still point of ritual
lives curl fetal in contemplation
uncurl in sweet bounty
of motion and sensation.

Strong arms lift and descend
chisel strikes ice
rises up, clashes down
cuts wider, cuts deeper
into the frozen silence
into the frozen memory of water
until water arrives
seeps through
splashes up the sides of the hole.
Another smaller circle
boring further into the spiral.
This swell of motion
round moist center of being
here.

Ice patterns hypnotize
children stare face down
read cracks and bubbles

many shades caves and textures
winter crafts of water.
Play warm in the afternoon sun
skaters jump small mounds of snow
squealing to a stunning stop
faces prickled by wet shards
as one blade point comes down
spray of tiny chips flies up.

Everything here cool sharp as ice chips:
sun's legend, blinding reflection
hand auger biting into frozen water
fishing rig's metal tips stuck deeply
wet exposed fingers baiting the lines
pushing hooks through squirming minnows
smooth cold handle of the four-pronged spear
spear thrust shivers into body of fish
stinging stars tingle through numbed feet
and fish spots dart behind closed eyelids.

Now crowded together
on overturned buckets, folding chairs
or blocks of chopped wood.
Ragged army blanket hung at the door
covers slits of rebel light
one fabric veil between brilliance
and blackness.
Sitting hunch-shouldered in blackness
now watching and listening
as fire crackles softly in the barrel stove.
Fishers of fishers
gathered in the darkened ice shack.
Passing snacks whispered stories
and time between us.

How once a muskrat rose sleek to the surface
snapped inches from your hand
surprised you weren't a fish
as you were surprised
by his hungry fury.

Remember the broken-backed
pike who scarred your hand
when this house sat
two hundred yards off the south shore.

Finding old fish and faces
in the green black bottom.
Accounts sometimes muddied, silt-clouded
by sudden false spear throw.
Waiting the winter for clarity
knowing how it comes to water
when sediment settles.
Remembering even dark January lake
seems lighted by contrast;
our dim lives by ritual.

Remember the white fish
swimming just below the surface
racing for a taste of the bait.
A craving for wax worms
their downfall that winter.

Puppeting carved decoys
making wooden fish swim dip dive
across the length and width
of the rectangular hole
cut in the floor of the house
cut in the floor of ice beneath.

Necks stiff bending over
watching the weeds for movements
watching beyond the ice edges
waiting for a smooth long length
to be lured in by green painted scales
to follow the flash of tin fins.
All eyes concentrate on the water
epicenter, only lighted area
in our six by eight world.

Schools of minnows flutter in and out
curious sunfish and perch
swim to the flashing intruder
hover back up
turn tail and rudder their exit.
Watching the underwater drama
for the signal *fear*
to clear the small fry away.
Holding our breath for the entrance:
the big one cautious nervous
lingers at the edge of the hole
withholding full view,
or lurks at the bottom watching
just out of spear's reach.

No excess motion now
hardly a whisper
just a spear advanced to striking point
lowered slightly into water
as one hand and one wrist continues
the soft slow looping of the decoy
taunting tempting slightly advancing
trying to move the walleye
the bass the northern
into view into range.

It watches an eternity
then rises to the bait.
Or languishes endlessly
until we chance a difficult throw.
It suddenly flashes away, gone.
Or swims halfway in
almost—almost—
enough!
Seized by a sharp thrust
twisting on the prongs
pulled squirming from the water.

Held tail-up for a profile
admired for fight and size and color
measured for story.
Then dropped quickly outside the door
or buried elbow deep beneath the snow
made safe from village dogs.

Remember old Coots got nailed
betrayed by his black lab puppy
fish retriever
digging up the illegal catch
tossing frozen bodies like sticks
landing them toothmarked
at the feet of the warden.

Water resettles as we do
retelling each moment of the action.
Watching now with greater expectation
imagining shadow fish
dreaming lunkers
remembering the old ones.
Caught by the spear

or caught in story
we carry them from this snug burrow.

Stepping out into daylight
startled mole-blind
by the mass of bright white ice and snow.
Gasping, breathless
stunned like a fish taken out of water
by the solid reality of cold
the sudden blank largeness
of the lake.
Stumbling on clumsy feet
newly awakening to movement,
find dark silence has sharpened sound
to hear baying dogs, squawking crows.
And vision trades depth for distance—
see flat horizon dotted with smoke stacks
the twinkling of far off lights—
on the oh too human land.

This emergence.
Another strange exhilaration
joy fresh, unwarranted.
Seeking cause
in the stiff scattered bodies of fish
in the white ice now stained
time marked with blood and urine.
Cold settles like vapors
around our warmer bodies
steaming to define our edges.
We stand shaped now in air by relationship
the falling temperature talking of pattern.

And these things told, too
passing time
while winter waits
on water.

Passing Time

The kitchen has a small table.
Formica wood grain
metal legs splayed out at each corner—
where a transistor radio sits.
This ancient platform holds ritual
items of daily living stained and folded,
napkins newspapers and grocery lists
piled inconspicuously as history.

Mornings we gather
elbows planted
like tent poles beneath our chins,
all day rotating shifts
as dreamers and window sill watchers,
caught up in life's small dramas.
Outside fox squirrels and jays
battle each day in the pitifully scarred limbs
of one old soldier amputee box elder.

We are kitchen sentries on duty
and call out when company comes.
Biindigen.
Visitors keep coming in
the screen door revolving
like seasons of the moon.
Ode'mini-giizis
strawberry moon,
waatebagaa-giizis
leaves changing color moon.

Voices speak into half empty cups.
Biindigen. "Come on in."

Company chair sits waiting
beneath the teapot clock,
hand-painted wooden stepping stool
below the garden window,
doorway space
for standing or leaning.
It's crowded sometimes, but good for talking,
just right to gather within reach
of gingersnaps and stovetop coffee,
a place where fresh air blows in
through all the windows and the open door.

It's a cribbage kitchen.
Worn cards always ready
shuffled like players' faces
like cribbage boards through the years.
1972, carved deer antler.
1984, three-handed ace.
And the small spiral notebook
meticulously lists 28 hands,
double skunks, wins and losses.
Games waver and cross
the ghost space of memory,
cross like voices calling
and cards falling.
Fifteen two, fifteen four
and there ain't no more.
See one, play one.
1998, this low vision innovation:
huge twenty-four inch board
white rings circling

each thumb-sized peg hole.
That's a go.

II

My uncle Bill came visiting.
Sitting there by the fridge
three weeks ago in November.
Mother hunched on the company chair,
Muff by the toaster, Daddy in the middle,
and me perched on the stool.
Muff brought me a war club.
We passed it by the diamond willow handle
admiring it and making jokes.

Then Bill was talking ricing.
Naming his poling partner,
the lakes and rivers they paddled,
telling how long they stayed out,
how many pounds they harvested,
where they slept each night.
All those details
the husk around a kernel.
Do you ever just ache
for something
a sliver of beauty
so tightly encased?
Dance dance the rice.

They had to come home early
he said
their car so small
no room for another day
another canoe bottom full

they had to come home
while still he longed to go out.
Bend and pound the rice.

Eighty-three this year,
he won't sell the rice.
Next season
he might not be able to go.
And him with so many
to support.
All us rice relatives.
Could he list us
like dependents
on his income tax?
Never once made enough
he laughs
to pay taxes.
Manoominike-giizis, ricing moon.

He ended the rice talk then
telling about a certain place
pretty place down by Mille Lacs.
It got dark early that day.
They had to turn back at the narrows
never got to rice the beds
beds they knew were just there
through the narrows
just there on the next lake.
"If I feel like I do now," he said,
"I'll go again."
Winnow with your every breath.

My Auntie came that day.
I gave her the stool

passed her the war club.
We were talking about birds now
about the two great horned owls
I kept stumbling upon last spring.
I was sneaking up on one
with my camera
and baby behind me
him imitating everything I did
when we got within ten feet
he took off running toward it
yelling
"Quack! quack! quack."
For him every bird was still a duck.

We all had bird stories to tell
that morning
in the time of the freezing moon
while my hair was drying
and I was drinking coffee
and my little dying mother
sat smiling
beneath the teapot clock.
Gashkadino-giizis.

STUDIES IN MIGRATION

Of Landscape and Narrative

*A story draws on relationships in the
exterior landscape and projects them onto
the interior landscape.*

BARRY LOPEZ

I

Boundary Waters Canoe Area Wilderness
one white flash
of recognition
and gone
snowy egret
dressed for breeding
shaggy neck plumes
jutting out
woodpecker silhouette

Colorado River, California
egret egret egret
native to two landscapes
collected in casual clumps
forage in shuffle steps
line dancing
to flush their prey

II

Brooks Range, Alaska
breath of caribou
passing within feet
of my longing

I watch each precise
setting of antlers
bull thrusting
high   this weight
of balance

small brindled calf
muzzle open in panic
bleating my presence
indifferent cow
grazing
belly filled
with knowledge
of journey

III

Jasper–Pulaski Wildlife Refuge
against October sky
red-headed skeletons
cranes all bone
and histrionics
parachute into fields
dusk quiet slashed
with awe and tremoloo

where sandhills gather
flocks of spindly legs
fold and unfold
wings fan up
          and down
lifted like marionettes
in gangly dance

IV

Estes Park, Colorado
elk herds travel
      down from mountain
lounge at town's edge
browse ornamental shrubs
bed down
on groomed grasses
while hunting parties
search aimlessly

bull displays prowess
bugling   warns intruders
head down
stamps out a charge
ancient elk medicine
still holds
for king of rut

Studies in Migration

Pulled into Joe Olson's landing. Patterns of the past leaping before us like the frogs caught here for fishing. With the force of long history they return. Welling up in the iron scent of spring water. Pooling amid last fall's leaves. Slowly seeping into shoes worn through at the big toe.

Each year someone comes home. Pat moved in next to her dad. Von settled on Grandma's old land. Laurie Brown, gone since after the war, came back that same year as the trumpeter swans. Pelicans have been filtering in for seven summers. Today they fill the north quarter of South Twin. The evening lake black with birds.

Each space held for years in stories. Waiting. Now reclaimed. *Your name was never empty.* We could have told them. *We kept it full of memories.* Our land the color of age.

Clouded titles fill courthouse files. But spring sap spills out just the same. Boiled in family kettles. Cast iron blackened over decades of fires. Some walk these woods seeking surveyors' marks. Some fingers trace old spout scars.

And flight the birds could tell us is a pattern. Going. And coming back.

Tracks and Traces

Days after the storm I walk back into the small woods. Early after-
noon sun flashing, winking off knee-deep winter snow. I stretch, take
awkward, too-long steps following large waffle-bottom boot prints.
Then find a gait — one lower foot in the path, one breaking a new
crust of snow. Cold crystals fall into my mukluks where they gap
open at the top. Snow tingles down my calves. Soon I switch to deer
paths. Following these I begin to read the stories, tiny tracks and traces
of birds, rabbits, mice. Delicate dustings skitter across the snow's
surface. Disappear into hidden tunnels. Lift off in flight. The deer
runs lead me beyond the human paths, deeper into winter, into finer
snow tales. Feather fans splay wide in descent onto prey. Raccoon
hands shovel, forage after food. Still hunting too, I fashion a walking
stick from a fallen hickory branch. Move smoothly now, following
the four-leggeds. Glancing back, I see my own three-footed im-
prints. Exhilarated, I know I am half-way there.

Lines from an Autumn Litany

In the smoky gauze of dusk
sheep at pasture bend to graze.
Mounds of tattered fleece
thick necks rounded toward the ground
scattered amid bales of discolored hay
amid curved humps of field stone.
Three species of gray yellow heaps
arch upon the flat back of earth,
merge in their reality,
flock one into another
until sight can no longer distinguish
sheephayorstone.

Dried fists of fall leaves
scatter across township roads
while drivers brake
for the blurred brown motion
of squirrels across their path.
Bunches of leaves rise up
lift off
like carrion-seeking crows.
So many patterns form
and disintegrate with autumn's breath:
oak mice, aspen opposum,
maple leaf pheasant.

Colored and shaped by air gusts
each moment
on the verge of transformation.
We are something else.

We are more truly ourselves.
And with the brush of night
we are all of one darkness.

What the Sun Has Left of Amber

I

Small tawny dog
lounges against my curled legs.
My curled legs
nestle amid tall autumn grasses.
Green, wheat gold, rust,
tawny.
My hands run over and over her coat
the grasses
the sun's reflection there.
Smoothing, soothing, scratching,
Sighing release through my palms.
Sun rays, autumn breath
fingercomb
my auburn hair.
Or is it my own hands
upon the veins
of every fallen leaf?

II

Writing here.
Is it for you
a gift?
Or for me
who has so much to learn?

Every movement stirs me
awake
to watch listen

wonder or sing refrain.
But I never could discern
one
single
direction.
Of energies.

III

My hair
grows rich.
Gold
like the grasses
like the sun
like the tongue caresses
of a tawny dog across my hands.
My hands lost
now
deep in autumn.
Strands of vision
entangled like grasses
in my hair.

IV

And later.
Seeking what the sun has left
of amber.
I shall pull words through
like fingers.

Imprints in Blackfeet Country

for Amethyst First Rider

Oldman River
Elbow Falls
Napi's body spirit
whirling like Trickster breath
like story wind
rounding the coulees
shaping earth like voices
Napi's form
written in the landscape
mapping
inhabiting
with warm Chinook memories
the home country
of every telling.

A Wash

mustard yellow forsythia
purple crocus
tender shoots poke green from moist dark earth

Dutch brilliant tulips
delicate pink-petaled apple blossoms
wild violets burrowed in lush new grasses

April eggs gathered in medley of hues:
muted brown, turkey soft green or robin blue
speckled or spotted in camouflaged color

irises, orchids, lupine, nodding trillium
green umbrellas of may apples
bold sun yellow daffodils

burst of lilac butterflies,
sum of striped bumblebees
flurry of fluffy dyed chicks

gold finches flock to feeder
black eared lambs to ewes

fields profuse with dandelions
hearts with the pallet of spring

Students of Scat

Pellets bumpy
like mulberries,
peanut-shaped
porcupine droppings,
black winding
braids of mink.
SCAT!
Some droppings
say exactly that.
Territorial animals
marking their range.

Leavings
on fallen logs
atop rocks, at tree base.
Following the pathways
looking for sign
seeking stories in scat.
Abundant brown marbles
number the waabooz.
Bunches of bullets
say deer use this meadow.

Scat like good gossip
whispers your whereabouts.
Straining to hear,
dissecting like sentences
these symbols of your presence.
Fat berried sausages
write coyote's menu-du-jour,

Bee's wings, fur,
tiny bones of mice
label skunk's dark passing.

Tracing each pattern.
Finding where badger burrows,
or raccoon fishes.
Who climbs the apple tree
and who's eating who.
Nature's census takers:
she with her nose
me with my eyes
my dog and I
devoted students of scat.

A Sequel

for Lenny

Butterflies
of yellows, rusts and browns
hairstreaks, admirals, swallowtails,
monarchs migrating
through our years together.
Colors and sizes
of time.
Fluttering like heart beats
uncounted beneath chest walls.
Marriage—
a bounty of butterflies
spiraling across our near vision,
and winters white with waiting,
listening.
Until fragile wings
beat
return
anew
round of joy.
And yes, they sing.
By faith love flies
and we by love.

zen for traveling bards

I

headlights search the fog
for any point of reference
while one foot rides the brake
find litter of small gone bodies
swerving I recall your voice
just go the true pace

in panic I flash my brights
the cloud white swallows more road
lone rabbit quicksilver streak and safe
let the night harbor its own
my hand clicks down to dim

II

learn to wait for poems this way

fill words with small sure lights
and follow them home

Haiku Seasons

I. AUTUMN

Hoof prints in soft clay
hollowed by fine deer potter
still holding night rain.

Downy woodpecker
sidles up shag bark hickory
tat-tatting for food.

Geese black silhouettes
tangled tracery of trees
sketch fall gothic skies.

II. WINTER

Pine weighted with snow
one branch launches white burden
springs up down, waving.

Juncos line the branch
slash marks on the calendar
counting days till spring.

Yesterday's snowman
how soon folds weeping to earth
gravity of warmth.

III. SPRING

Four fluffed doves
plump line on snowy branch
tin drip of spring thaw.

Language of droplets
ping ponging gutter downspouts
overheard spring nights.

On May's brown plowed earth
only swaying black neck stems
honking into dusk.

IV. SUMMER

Thumbnail size tree frogs
rise, scatter like popping corn
fill my morning walk.

Birch limbs over lake
leaves shimmer reflected light
turn green silver green.

Fat pile of puppies
tangled in afternoon sun
sleep until hungry.

V. INFINITY

Many times I glimpse
feeding bird or clump of earth
one returns my look.

EVOLUTIONS

March 1995: Seeking Remission

Now I shall count the years
like rabbits.
Cottontails
flashing zigzag white trail
through barren woods.
Longlegs, jackrabbit,
hind-stepping high and quiet
into hiding.
And those brown rabbits
who sit quietly before me
hoping I do not see.
Those white winter furs
twitching so slightly
with rabbit breath.
Waabooz Spirit.
I hold each sign
a blessing.
And now I shall treasure
as vision
each brown season
each white.
And maybe the seventh year
will come
with life
as plentiful
as rabbits.

March 1998: Seeking Solace

Mother, Auntie, Grandma, Marlene,
we believe you inhabit these lands.
Your spirit embedded here
blowing like Bass Lake breezes
across our fish-wet hands.
Pushing up moccasin flower shoots
along the Tamarack trails.
Casting before us scents
we know to be our relatives
cedar, pine, and sweetgrass.
Etching story words and pictures
in white-gray birch bark patterns.
Calling names in the language of birds
Nay-tah-waush, Mah-no-men
Gaa-waababiganikaag.

And we leave here now
dreaming White Earth dreams.
Scarlet flames of sumac,
soft green fronds of fern;
colors nudge dark edges of despair.
And we leave here now
bearing close, round images of home.
Of hummingbird's nest and family markers,
large brown Antell eyes,
twice delicate abalone vision:
Earth mounds like fallen breasts,
soft moss of women's cleft lives.
Hallowed here by wailing wolf orphans

voices form like dew at dusk at dawn
moist with treasure, hoarse with desire.

Night webs, filters of howling darkness,
catch and sift our dreams, feed us peace.
Woven labyrinth, source of warm rest,
your healing feather drips chip through,
melt deathly cold winter-ice loneliness.
Now lips in sleep move with prayer breath
ripple the soft down underside of ducks.
And we sign ourselves followers
of alloted land and lives;
And we sign ourselves followers
of Bunkers, Browns, Antells and Blaesers.

Another Midnight Flute

Moist May by moonlight
Sound of distant train whistle
Keening your absence

Stand in spring moonlight
Crickets sound voices of lonely
Singing along.

Kitchen Voices

I

In the crowded rooms of childhood
listening.
Your voices
the familiar lullaby
punctuating the world
from one door away.
Hobby horse dreams
waltzing to the tones of meaning
behind the muffled words.
Hearing Hank Snow crooning
beneath the kitchen clatter
and sizzle of midnight hamburgers.
Tennessee Ernie Ford singing background
for your version
of "The Old Rugged Cross."
Sounds
lapping against the shore
of my knowing
of my sleep.

Evenings spent eavesdropping
on pickle jars popping
as they cool and seal,
Santa's mad wrapping frenzy
on Christmas Eve.
The play by play
of Cassius Clay
and Sonny Liston
mingles with beer bottles

and late night laughter.
Sometimes wires cross
and Saturday-night fights
start in the kitchen.
Your voices crashing
heedless angry waves
wear themselves out
and stumble off to bed.
In the sudden dark uneasy silence
counting heartbeats.
Then growls and pops of snoring
join the night howl
of the freight train.
The sunflower farmers'
staged gunshots
bark in the distance.
These moving tides of sound
bearing me though the years.

Every slumber woven with vibrations.
Chair legs scraping the floor,
ice cubes cracked from their trays,
tips tinkling together
coins counted and dropped
into the giant Seagram's bottle bank.
Shadows cross
the narrow stream of light
beneath the door of my room
or my dream,
popcorn scents
puff through the keyhole.
Twin aches,
comfort and loss,
wake me again.

Torn between rising
to the night kitchen,
or letting the spell
of unreality
lull me like water. . .
Water running from the faucet
your day's stories flowing out
sometimes flooding the space between you.
Wanting despite everything
to hear it forever.

II

In my childhood's bedroom
beside my own deep-dreaming baby
resting together in one hollow
of the age-worn mattress.
Listening again—and still.
Floors creak beneath your tired step
cupboard doors pop open snap closed
grocery sacks crack along their folds
and you sit shuffling cards between you.
Mingled with these
sound pictures
carry from other rooms and years.
My breath always coming and going
with the motion of your voices rising
and whispering themselves away.
Waiting now,
child rustling the bed beside me,
humming soothing his Morphean visions
careful never to disturb my own.
Twin dreams with only a door between them.
One spun of longing of need

for old voices to speak on and on
to ferry me across time on their currents.
Fearing your life song will fall silent
and with it the pendulum of meaning.
Too quiet nights will stop my ears
my speech, my joy.

Huffs of child warm breath on my arm
trace like voices the buried vein patterns
born of blood and devotion
from the bed hollow of sound and history.
Softly here I try my voice
cooing the story of years
years shaped by the wash
of womb sounds breaking against sleep.
Rest, baby, in this room made of memories
still now, my heartsounds patter against yours.
Listening, again, as from a distance
certain I am the voice of his slumber
knowing truly it is my cadence and range
that sings to this child a known world.
And that it is but a simple translation
of those ageless kitchen voices
chanting lives
chanting from the far side of my soul
sha sha sha shaaa
and *follow me.*

III

In the locked house of memory
old spirits rise, sing rockabye.
Rounded vowels soften our sleep
oohing like pine wind

sweeping though our dreams
stardusting us with longing.
Lingering traces hibernate
in soundless sleep,
until whining cicada summers
toss us awake
hot sweating
waiting for footsteps
for thunder drumming.
Twilight, starlight, moonlight, midnight,
dusky hours of deep dark.
Nap, nod, drowse,
sink to soft rest and surface
always to the subtle base
background rhythm of kitchen nightlife.
In these muted echoes of night
is formed our daylight.
January moon's
too bright light
crackles along winter air
with sharp undercurrents of sound.
Static, sulfur smell of a match
just scratched awake,
splat of a flyswatter,
a cough, a sneeze
one final yawning, *Sweet dreams*,
and *Turn out the light*.

Letting Go

for George and Nancy Benton

I sit in comfort
nestled in your chair
before a fire you have built
drinking from a mug
marked with your name: Nancy.
Marked like this place
with scents and stories
with the trappings of your lives.
I watch as you leave them now
not like animal leavings
to ward off intruders,
but a gentle legacy.

How graciously you pass things on
like a lovely holiday pudding
sent round the table.
And quietly you list:
extra linen in the closet,
a full collection of spices,
lantern wicks top drawer.
a set of French Classics
for rainy-day reading.
I listen as you instruct:
how to start the generator
with the power off
so it's not calling for a load;
how to squelch the CB,
fill the propane tanks,
snap and lock the trundle beds,
light each pilot light and heater.

Then with ageless long-legged grace
you descend the stairs,
and delicately you point
touch the vacant space
the gap between the boards
separating the last step and the walkaway.
This ghost spot, tiny cleft in time
in time will house a wild orchid.
Just here the Round-leaved Orchis
blooms again each year.
Blooming as you have
in some gap of time or space
just here
on the point
of the small bay
on the north side
of Farm Lake.

Now you recite
as if it were a bedtime rosary
names and relationships
of long-time lakehome residents,
a list of newcomers
their origin and occupations.
With yawning arms you point
the locations of resorts
and garbage dumps.
Hum rituals of care and cleaning
familiar as old camp songs.
Identify the propane supplier,
the brand name of the composting agent
Quick John to use in the outhouse.

As you ladle the information
I grow dizzy
not from the minutiae I must remember
but from the rotations of the moon
I see in your eyes
from the tiny crackings of your heart
as it pulses one more time
around each fine-carved piece, each memory,
holds and then releases
the worn pages of bird books
bright tulip-patterned dishes
chair arms
puzzle games
the dinner bell
caressing objects as incantations
calling sounds
from twenty years past
gently letting go
with each storied item
moment by moment
this era from your life.

Two long-time comrades
settled in your companionship
side by side
year by year
now affectionately
you share the remembering,
bit by bit
piecing together details
of building and furnishing
and childrearing
a changing roll of names
of fishing holes and trophy catches.

The routines here
mapreading and handstitching
so satisfying to perform
clearing brush and trellis gardening
satisfying to tell and to hear.
Each departing step creaks out more
dock sounds and water lapping
tell them still when you are gone.

In my sleep I play Goldilocks
to the cottage and porridge and chairs.
The bed does not fit right,
the pillow, the blanket.
This time it's the moose who come home:
Someone has been living in my cabin!
And here she is wondering
if in the aftermath of your going
each tinkle of silverware
each whistle of the tea kettle
the clatter of pots and pans
will sound like laughter
will echo voices of old friends
who stopped here once
who sang and toasted
and pan fried fish.
And your voices?
And ours following you?
Will they join chorus
sing welcome
to those rustles of time past?

And when you have gone
leaving us with your blessing
I touch small pieces of your lives

as if they are sacred objects
instead of just canvas gloves
left to dry on pegs
above the big wood stove.
I place hearty northwoods snacks
pippin apples and granola bars
on the wicker tray
at the far right end of the counter
as you have done for years.
I sing lullabies to this place
as if it were a lonely child
whose mother has gone away.
And I wonder if I can learn
and if the cabin will teach me
and if the lake will soothe me
and I wonder if twenty-five years
of Boundary Water breezes
blowing by and by
will be enough time
to study the Orchis art
of blooming
then letting go.

Evolutions

I

At night
passing by
watching life
in each lighted window.
My heart
strains to hear
Mick Kelly's
lonely music.
Me
hunting, too
for something
more
more tangible
than baby grand
gleaming
in round window alcove.

Reading
the stories
of those houses
in snatches
of green flowered wallpaper
heavy beige fabrics.
Counting their riches
in book-lined shelves
in Santa suits at Christmas.

Counting mine
in treasured designs
engravings
fine etchings
of memory.
Passing by
with you
at night
on the streets
of Billings
of Dickinson.
Feeding our visions.
The white puffs of breath
escaping on the fall air.
Finding music
in the spiraling tones
of your voice,
riches
in the gleam
of your storied eyes.

III

Turning,
leaves
to color,
your face
to lines,
to graying,
to ghost puffs of memory,
to vision.
At night
passing by

your face
in the darkened window
of a dream.
A reflection
of visions
turning over
like centuries,
of lives
turning over.
Evolutions.

your old lost loves

for I have left
the same handsome men
standing in photos
with that girl
from my past
seeing them grow younger
leaner, taller
each year
hearing their deep
fine words
in the rustle
of each fall's leaves

together
barefoot
we walk
country roads
ankle deep in mud
I turn to you
young laughing ghost
hubba hubba
never quite matching
your daring
ooh la la
I need those memories
fourteen kids
and no papa

some lovers I know
in stories
some by heart
for I stand
just as you did
on the same lake shore
watching darkness come
suns setting in unison
casting long shadows
one after another
across the years

old lost loves
you and I
clasping identical dark hands
smelling of clay and damp pine
hearing again
song of owl and loon
endless and lonesome
lingering night sounds
bouncing
echoing forever
back and forth across
a single lake
called time

Passing St. Kilian's

Old country steeple
Tombstones tumble down the hill
Side with eternity.

Old country steeple
March grave heaped in my mind
Woodland ephemerals.

MOTHERBIRTH

Fetal Disposition

It's time you were heading south
they say.
Finding the errant head
cupping the tiny buttocks
and changing your direction.
Within my dark watery womb
you slide easily around
find your sucking finger
and bide your time.

One turning follows another.
Each time
the weight of your small form
beneath my swollen abdomen
shifts
alters my center
my pact with gravity.
But each time
determined
you flip back
with an Antell stubbornness
I secretly cherish.

You may not have breath
but you have such will.
And soon they learn
you don't take orders
won't be turned
from your fetal intuition

that keeps you
feet down
ready to hit the earth running.

motherbirth

small scuttled breaths
warm about my neck
squeaks
whimpers
sighs
tiny newborn cries
in my dreams
that waken
here in half-dark room

rabbit light
falls across your bed
between your sleep
and mine
between my old worn life
and this new dream
I stand
half afraid
of both

canal of indecision
floating
as if to choose

but you cry out
here
in this one place
and I with you
bound now
swaddled
moving to your rhythms

swaying, rocking
cooing womb song
I hear my voice
intone heartbeats
soothing each
waking
changing
feeding
sleeping

light slides round
our days
time breathes
baby breath
slowly in and out

so new
the sound of you
but sure
as your hunger
cries red-faced
from flannel wrapped wings
eyes glistening
tiny wide mouth
pulling me in
holding me
suckling
grounding me
force beyond gravity
old as time
but fresh again

Gavin
tiny White Hawk
winter night and I
welcome you

Baby Pantoum

Now I lay you down to sleep
Hush now, hush now my little son,
Pray you please the quiet keep
Now that this long day is done.

Hush now, hush now my little son
Diaper dry and just now fed,
Now that this long day is done
It's high time you went to bed.

Diaper dry and just now fed
You've heard each song I know in turn,
It's high time you went to bed—
Ah, there must be other lullabies to learn.

You've heard each song I know in turn
Played peek-a-boo and patty cake,
Ah, there must be other lullabies to learn.
Or some new parent class to take.

Played peek-a-boo and patty cake,
Rushed to wash and dry and fold;
Some new parent class to take,
With this little mind to mold.

Rushed to wash and dry and fold
Mashed bananas, baked fresh bread,
With this little mind to mold
There's never time to rest my head.

Mashed bananas, baked fresh bread.
And wondered again did I do alright?
There's never time to rest my head.
And when will he sleep the night?

And wondered again will I do alright
Winter's ginger-haired baby child?
And will you ever sleep the night?
Sun has set and evening's mild.

Winter's ginger-haired baby child,
Pray you please the quiet keep.
Sun has set and evening's mild,
Now I lay you down to sleep.

fragments from a
mother's journal

I

huffs of your sleeping
breath a tiny bellows
blowing cool across my arm.

II

wiggles, giggles and grimaces
a marching parade of pouts
as dream chases dream
across your newborn face

blowing puppy snorts
peeps, gasps and gurgles
and mewing whispered purrs
each sound bursts from stories
you hear beneath your rest.

III

cat birds at the sill
and you beside me
shrill calls each morning.

lilting vowel songs
following your happiness
up and down the scale
on each new octave you discover.

chasing every joy with notes
singing it soundly
in endless variation
fluttering baby keyboard
of fingers and toes

your voice more mobile
then your four-month body
and dimpled like your cheeks.

IV

pink fledgling mouth
popping wide and holding patient
milk bliss feeding us both.

V

plum-sized fists and berry toes
each of your fingers and mine
into the choir-boy O
sweet hollow of your mouth.

velvet tongue traces
discovering tastes and shapes
memorizing each
and wetting them with life.

Don't Burst the Bubble

Outside with his Daddy
he runs back
soap solution in his hand
because he thinks
I am the magic.
Only Mommy
can throw round rainbows in the air
cover the grass with glass bulbs
only Mommy
can tickle beauty from her lips
coax it through the wand
until it multiplies
and rushes out
translucent
only Mommmy
can blow bubbles
that tease his chase
floating fleeing
popping at his touch.
He thinks the magic is me.
Please don't tell him
it's really Fisher Price.

Up-Ducky-Down

You turn the world
"Kitty-up, kitty-up!"
with your call.
Gleefully rocking my heart,
your wooden *neigh-neigh*,
the stodgy sense of sounds —
goes *up-ducky-down*.
And mystery and attachment
rent space in our house
count as you do
wy, shoe, shoe, wy shoe.
Identities, Imeyou
swittling together.
"Mama carry you!"
While *big grrr, little grrr*
and tigrr
keep changing their clothes
kissing their reflections
"he backwards"
and clapping their hands.
Each emphatic
Sa! Sa
and every deliberate pout
Wi wi woo!
translates a tumbling village
of childhood
to lonesome expatriots
and the fiddlefaddle pellmell followme
language that jumps on your bed
returns somersaulting alphabets

and poetry.
And when the *wow-wow*
slides down *whee* and lands *ta-da*
in the lap of your memory
ambition goes up-ducky-down:
"Now you turn go kitty-up"
and I do.

Beyond Measure

I

Five feathers deep
and as tall as the moon.

More than all the pages
in all the books
in the whole world.

This is the size
of your love
when you are four
and you have
cherry popsicle swimming
in your blue blood.

II

Until Alaska's summer sun
turns in early.

Until I can memorize the names
of all the women who
have ever held children
against their breasts
in every century
in every country
on this whole turtle earth.

This is how long
you will love

when you are a mother
of a child four
who sings sugary songs
induced by nothing more
than a popsicle
and your presence.

From Memory's Daybook

Back like a child's ghost.
This sky of old gone days
home to twinkling star tales
and banana moons.

Sing-song greetings
Hey Man in the Moon!
Ain't seen you since
ain't see you clear
ain't ever see you like that
first time.

Lifted cheek to cheek
following the line of grown-up finger
pointing the milky way to your face:
carved marshmallow features
against yellow-orange roundness
against Crayola midnight blue.

Peering with cat eyes
through open barn doors,
following *once upon a time*
to the crater of your mouth.
Riding story words like gold
on the tails of lightning bugs.
Finding your magic far off world
sinking my teeth into the green cheese
of recitation.

Hey, Man in the Moon
where you been lately?

This Song

Norway's arrow into fall dark sky
pine needles pillow my arm
which pillows your head
which roots against my breast
until we settle suckling and nesting
on the forest floor.
And it starts just at the moment
that my milk lets down
the soft howling ache of windsong
a lonesome caress of sound
through waving tree tops.
Late September blowing,
a fiddler's bow across branchstrings
singing of some distant home
crooning vowels of ancient lullabies.
Blanketed by this ghostly loon chorus
together beyond ordinary breath or time,
the pulse of your lips against my nipple
the rising rushing sound of souls
passing, the falling away of words.

FROM ONE
HALF MAD
WRITER TO
ANOTHER

Hat Tricks

for the Word Warriors

It's something you do with sounds
pulling them like filmy silks
one after another after another
from the illusion of bottom
until they stream forth
like singing rivers of color
lifting voiceaftershapeaftersoundafter
endless alphabet scales
falling up in serpentine spirals
of beauty.

It's something you do with words
sculpting them from the clay of silence
joining their dictionary bodies
until nouns couple
tumble over verbsadverbsconjunctions
molding them together
until they take form
under the wand of your muse
rise up as rabbits or birds
magic or truth.

It's something you do with hollowness
the empty dark container of self
absence turned inside out with longing
nothing up my sleeve
endlessly probing the void of the unwritten
searching for language, vision, incantation
to unlock the tongue

cut the strings of reluctance
that hold stories back
captured in the black hat of negative space
until spoken they come untethered
escape levitate in the ecstasy of expression
and you fill each aching absence
with poetry.

letter, from one half mad writer to another

for Lorne Simon

Poets, you said
eating watermelon
that hot July in Norman
peel off old skins.

My mouth
cracked at the corners
and those useless layers
dropped away with each word.

Nothing, you said
as you left
for summer travel
ever decays
for the Poet.

One stray image stays:
The gallery yard filled
with gnats and 500 Nations.
And that tree
where we leaned
laughing in shadows,
in shadows
dusk handsome bark
becomes Micmac.

Only the skin, you said
in your letters

from B.C.
of things decays.

Only the skin
I repeat to myself
as I trace your name
in an ink scrawl,
your presence in a signature.

Poems, you wrote,
draw memory
like moon power
pulls on the seas
and creates tides.

Now your voice calls back
pulls from *Skedeg'moochv-outi,*
the Road of the Spirits,
the Milky Way.
Words scattered like breadcrumbs
to find our way from madness home.

Moon soft rhythms,
The Poet's voice, I say,
drawing water
on a journey of memory
where two half mad writers
become one.
And tide rises
and tide falls away.

Where Vizenor Soaked His Feet

White Earth, Itasca, Walker,
Pine Point, St. Benedict's Mission,
The Northwest Angle, Bemidji,
Cass Lake, Franklin Avenue.

Shadows cast
by your history
in this country.
Agawaatese.
Linger like your presence
along my pathway
wavering beckoning
at the treelines.

Your words echo
mingle laughter
in the voice of crows
in the *ha ha ha haaaa*
of bear.
The *story in your blood*
now deep in mine.

Twice and thrice told
four-fold tricksters
Harold of Orange
Griever the American Monkey King
Almost Brown
and Clement Beaulieu.
Tricksters of Liberty
chase tragic dancers

strip tease decode
secret intellectual societies
walk backwards
burn *luminous* with dreams.

Survivance your legacy.
Wild tales, colorful crossbloods,
humor howling from the pages,
lusty like reservation dogs.
Liberation, imagination,
healing story medicine
in your deep bass voice.
Riding chance
on the *Naanabozho Express.*

Bass Lake, Bad Medicine,
Little Elbow, Gull Lake,
On the shoreline
lost and lonesome.
Wewebanaabii.
She is fishing.

North Twin, McCraney,
Rock Lake, Strawberry Lake,
Skipping stones like stories
Dangling toes for the minnows.
Feeling a tug, a tickle,
trickster nibbling at my dreams.
Agawaatese, a shadow presence
in these places
where Vizenor soaked his feet.

Cerca de Aquí

I've wanted directions,
Direcciones.
A place I've searched for
where voices and people come together,
Like the four corners
Utah, Colorado, Arizona and New Mexico.
Cuatro angulos.
Like my life overlapping all the borders,
sitio converger.

Muy simple, no?
But I find my way so slowly
toward that place.

Habla despacio, por favor.
Each language so new
each people.

Estoy buscando
I am looking.
Can you tell me
es cerca de aquí?

Bilingual

I wake
fearing
I have forgotten
the single word
you taught me.

To love and to want.

Both together in a word
like a breath
like a moment.

Hugging the small pillow
to my breasts
I lay
straining
against forgetfulness
and fitful memory.

Tourist words
surface
in the dark
donde, dónde está
where, where is?
cuánto
how much?
no entiendo
I don't understand,
lo siento
no, not that
no regret.

Cómo se dice
How do you say?

Struggling to remember
desire, love
lost whispers
of a language
I had not known.
Qué pasa?
Qué es esto?

Puedo?

Por favor.

In longing
I recall
the single moment
I knew their merger.

And then the word
rises up
speaks itself
unbidden.

Into the dark:

Te quiero.

And Still You Refused
to be a Shaman

for Terry

Time and again
though I asked
by the weight of my head
my neck, my limbs
in your hands.

Though you read my history
in the divet on my tongue,
noted with studied vision
a deficiency in my lungs,
called it out loud by its name
palpitating that Sorrow
with your hands.

Even now you drive the needles
fingers tapping,
piercing at each point
the tightness —
scarred memory we call skin,
then spinning each silver axis in turn
to waken,
fire with pain,
the knotted tissues of time.

How can you
who burns with stories,
blows their incense

moxibustion
into the fragile openings
of my body,
resist this plea?

You wear the cinnamon eyes
of the people,
your dusty past selves
float within each marbled orb.
And I know purple memory
pulses,
racing through pathways
of your bulging warrior veins.

Therefore, *Mashkikiiwinini,*
won't you sing just once
let the rising pitch
of your medicine voice
puncture the shroud,
deeply held silence of loss,
now chanting
call forth energy like remembrance
drumming *chi*
with echoes of ancient sound?

Night Tremors

You call late and early.
All night long
I hear the sound
of your confusion.
My own
waking now
in the silence
that you left
on the line.
A confusion
no cheery a.m. D.J. chatter
can dispel.

We orchestrate our own pain.

Find the places
that hurt
most,
test our tolerance
new ways
each passing year.

Probe
each safe nest
of belief,
hold to science
each trembling
new born
intuition,
test the strength
of love.

Your voice like Fernando's
wanting that profession
that would keep him alive,
like my own betraying whimper
seeking assurances
which no other soul can give,
like each lost voice
waking alone
still calling out at night
for a glass of water
a lullaby, a story
for someone to turn on the light
to check under the bed for monsters.

How safe?
we wonder
and must know.
How real, long, firm,
good, true—
how safe?
will you make my life
or keep it.

That we must
each
safeguard
our own
destiny
I resist.
And so I will still
call out
and will listen
to each cricket voice
confess

his longing
all night
in the moist dark.
Waking again
sore and stiff
from the pain
that I have borne
inside.

Perhaps it is true
and finally
I must learn.
There are limits
to all things
to safety and to pain.

A phone ringing in the dark
is no more than any night sound
and must be left alone
like the sounds of wolves howling
coyotes yipping
frogs croaking
or humans weeping.

lament

for all the wild young girls
spitfires
branded
ridden
like rodeo broncos
through Mainstreet
for spectacle.
spurred out of the chute
as long as you live in my house

young lady
whipped passionate
by forbidden young men
in ponytails.
bucking curfews
homework
high school dress codes.

spray painting
class of nevermind
coloring sarcasm
in Avon
sweet cherry lipstick
Cover Girl
blue danube eye shadow
and Max Factor
apple candy blush.

tossing manes
like Rapunzel

out every window.
the ladder up
streaked by sun and lemon.
tossing back
and back
Blatz
strawberry Boones Farm
and peppermint schnapps.

for all the giddy-
up girls
standing in midnight dew
at country kegs
and blowing their youth
out their nostrils:
smoke signals
few would understand
or return.

Saturday hickies
hidden beneath Sunday
turtlenecks worn like bridles
tamed,
hunched guilty,
waiting,
to make another
break for it.

days passed
in slow recitations
writing *I will not*
a hundred times
reading home-ec *recipes*
for a happy marriage

slip covering
layer upon layer
over the stains
of lust
like blinders blocking daylight
smothering
memory
and longing.

for all the prancing youth-
fullness of time
has come undone
and women harnessed
forget their firebrand
madness.
and dance,
now finely choreographed
like Lipizzans
of haute ecole,
a waltz of age.

is this how?
wild girls
become their mother's
clone.

for all the vanished rebels
spending quiet guilt
forgetting
small infractions
of youth,
the smell of musk,
and joy.
for all the tired women

wearing life
like some virus they caught
whose incubation
was twenty years.

Are you sure Hank done it this way?

for Craig Womack and all the C & W Ind'ns out there

Plucking old country songs
on a borrowed guitar
with a broken e-string.
Rusty thirtysomething voices
whining wailing
toward midnight —
You'll cry and cry. . .
the whole night through.
Riding glottal stops
and grace notes,
flying your musical time machine,
remembering
everything
but the lyrics.
Sounding
singing ourselves
out of that room
on word chants
words like ancient rituals
we longed for
just out of our reach
like youth —
Why don't you love like you used to do?
How come you treat me like a worn out shoe?
Making music like some things matter
still
bending those strings those notes
into shapes
we almost recognize.

Sparking chords
that glow like animal eyes.
Voices burning fast patterns
like sparklers
sounds exploding fireworks
into the smoky darkness
of long gone bayou memories—
Please release me
Let me go
For I don't love you
Anymore.
Linked like quarter notes
hands on one another's shoulders
swaying
paper dolls strung out
on laughter.
Holding tunes like reins
steering ourselves
clear
through 500 years of history —
Poor old Kawliga
He don't know what he missed.
Conjuring off-key harmony
feet tapping
fingers snapping
beating time like owl's wings
on moist night air,
who-whooing our own call.
Last lonely laments
criss-crossing voices
camping out on the edge of everything known.
Nowaday quests.
Songs
surfacing around us like faces

ancient enemies swooping like hawks
crayon colored fantasy friends of childhood
old wrinkled grandmas
and bolo-clad granduncles,
gathering together
drawing us into their spinning visions
centering us finally
in vibrating sound,
an arrow
off taut bowstring
shot straight at the heart —
Six days on the road
and I'm gonna make it home tonight.

THOSE THINGS
THAT COME
TO YOU
AT NIGHT

Anza Borrego, 1995

Grace wavers
like memory,
a fragile uncertainty.
The mapping
of ephemeral streams
on desert terrain,
witnessed
by faint marks
across the land,
read by faith.
The history of a wash
waiting
to be filled.

One surprise rain
colors rock and sand.
Desert rain
filling each crevice
of pain packed earth.
Waking scent
yucca and creosote,
teasing out
small blossoms.
Tiny rivulets
of freedom
trickle down,
run overflow
finding
ancient paths
washing them clean
of history's debris.

Palm oasis
hidden mid-mountain
on rocky treks.
Shades of green and blue
amid dusty grays and browns.
Cool pools of grace
soothing.
A chimera
sighted
like silhouettes
of big horn sheep
on distant peaks.
Once a mirage
watery illusion
shimmering hope
in every hot sun
a trick of vision
or light
pursued to death
by every lost traveler.

But listen.
What they have never named
cannot claim
survived here
on roots
and cactus milk.
Jack rabbit terrain
cracked open in thirst.
Morteros,
hollowed bellies of rocks,
fill now
with rain and memory.
Oh Kumeyaah and Cahuilla,

Oh desert dwellers
of earth or spirit,
all ephemeral voices
of this America,
echo here.
Each hollow lie
of history
waits to be filled.
And now we send our words
to fall
like snow
in the desert.

In the Tradition of
the Peacemakers

*For Robert Blaeser, sworn in as District
Court Judge August 21, 1995.*

Put on robes like garments of peace
wear them
heavy with history
long they join you to earth
and full
to harbor beneath their folds
all voices, all shapes and sizes of vision.

Put on robes like feathers
and wear them
a symbol of honour
and duty
wear wisdom and compassion
wear justice like a rainbow
all colors
a promise.

Fill your robes with traditions
a will to peace and not to power
speak voices of centuries
house in your heart
laws fragile with age
tend with your love
their roots
still bearing.

From your hands
dispense dignity
to each person.
Hold this office
like a medicine
like a ritual
to heal
to bestow human rights.

Now I hear your name
spoken by the elders.
Now you must go forward.
Burn cedar
prepare yourself
paint your face
like a warrior for justice.
Put on robes
enter the council
and join a league of peace.

Matrix

for Dorothy Davids, at 80

Northshore rocks stretch endlessly
beyond the limits of your vision,
like years
piled before eyes of a child.

Yet relentless in will
you pilgrimage
to gather
these sacred to you
treasured as the story of Rock Boy.
Sitting atop and among them
palming for weight
fingering each glacial orphan,
stone spirit.

Now I tell the story
of old mother bearing
rock children in leather pouches,
bestowing
these spirit gifts on Indian lives,
placing them
                    heavy
as honor
in their hands.

Granite quartz obsidian
lake cool and time polished smooth:
their alabaster bodies
                    turn over and over

on waves of time.
Here recall rushing falling power
                            of water.

They come from water,
so give them a drink now and then.

Encrusted grains of earth memory.
Shaped by age
pumice and human longing,
once craggy edges
curve into years,
marbled now
coming full circle to wisdom.

Their stories and yours
voicing roundness
as wrinkled hands cup themselves
close once around stone.

Of My Affections

for Maymie Antell

Fuschia.
White racer stripes
around the ankles.
Marked each with your *M.A.*

They flew
with me late at night
around the high school track,
Mahnomen mornings
along the silo road,
followed that summer
by ice cream bars
for breakfast.

Which is harder
to understand:
how they could have worn
through so quickly
at each heel,
or how I could wear
the same comfort
for eighteen years?

Is it really easier
to conjure up
the gray fringe of your braids
around your toothless laugh
when I attach
your tiny form to

feet shuffling pink
along hospital corridors?

How long would
anything last
were we to discard it
at the first sign of wear?
I prefer life
broken in
like my socks.

Those Things That Come to You at Night

"Old Woman, Grandmother," she said. "They come to me at night."
"What is it they want?"
"Can't tell. Ain't like I really hear them clear."

Like voices I've known
sounding off
over the hill
behind the milk shed
under the belly of a car
coming through the woods
familiar tones and rhythms
like surface conversation
heard while underwater
the sliding pitch of sound
but no clear word borders.

"You must try to hear and remember. Sounds, pictures, the
stories they bring you, the songs."

Swimming among the fluid notions
of dream space
where voices land
in the hollow behind the house
and echo back to sleeping souls
where ideas ricochet
off of each documented waking moment
but strike home
in the slumbering core.

"They tell me things I'm sure. I want to get up to follow. But I can't pull my body along. When I wake up I am homesick for those voices. And then sometimes, maybe when I am hauling water or frying bacon, I remember something, just a feeling really."

*The old woman, bent over her basket, nods her head slowly. "Yes,"
she says. The younger one waits. Nothing more.*

Night speaking
touching spirit
without distinguishable words or voice
calling by name
calling your ancient being
arousing that felt destiny
waking all past
folding the torn moments together
and shaking them out whole.

"Grandmother?"
*"It's that way, child. The night things. Like how you learned to
walk. Nobody can teach you."*

Now a rumbling comes
heard over a heartbeat
beating more rapidly
with a fear of
greatness
felt in the bladder
breathed with flared nostrils
approaching like a flood
it rushes upon you
cleanses you with night desire
leaves you floating peacefully
into daylight.

"They get louder, I'm told."

"The voices?"

"Ayah. Louder if you don't seem to hear. Louder still until you hear or go deaf. Everybody has a choice you know. Some go night deaf. Others learn to listen."

Singing the songs
of midnight
going quiet, smiling shyly
when someone hears
listening inside
voices rounding each corner
of yourself
forming you
from dark light
remembering
those things
that come to you at night.

Meeting Place

I

Sweet garments of memory,
I don't know how to follow you.

Crossing and recrossing
the borders.

I was a mermaid once
for ten minutes
in a four-year-old's eyes
and became one
then
and now
when I remember
and emerge.

From the water
laughing
hair like seaweed.

Crowned princess, twice
one night in North Carolina
one in Illinois
my identity
so easy
Indian princess
the one in Peter Pan.

Refuses
like him
to grow old.

Simple distances those.

II

But these. . .

At the boat landings, I see you raise your leg, knee bent, stepping to shore. Your hair falls across my eyes. I tilt our chin and flick it back, then brush it away with the back of our hand because the fingers hold to the handle of the bucket. The hand is chapped and tight with the cold night air. It smells of fish.

Then you look up and I see you grin your triumph. I remember the tired joy we felt at bringing home a meal. But when we arrive, we see the game warden who took those fish we netted that hungry year. We zip up our thin jackets and rub our hands against our pant legs knowing we must try again and knowing he knew, too.

I pass the bucket to the eager children, reach down to grab the boat and pull her further onto shore. The old man grasps the other side, together we ease it out of the water. But as I turn to nod my thanks, shouting faces, angry twisted mouths, crowd in at the edges of the night. They are that frowning game warden of sixty years past. They are the resort owners' overgrown children, cursing, throwing stones.

You are stepping out of the boat. Your hair falls full across your eyes. When you push it back, I am standing before you, a protector. You are my past, standing before me. I am at the landing, one foot on shore, one in the shallow water.

Epilogue

The energy of poems constructs a community. Arising as they do from the whole of our experience, they are not ours to start. They come from a history we were born into, a collection of family names and accounts we have heard, a map of places we have traveled. They are sifted from music and books and dreams. Even in their writing they seek shape from an aesthetic older than our remembrance of it. Beyond this, their written life and their speaking continues only by the grace of and on the lips of other lives.

Whether we write our ancestry or our summer wanderings, the storywords throb with a backbeat. And so I thank the orchestra, the community alive in my poems. The people of Mahnomen and Nay-tah-waush. My writing comrades. My babies. Every story wind or skunk wind that has every blown my way. And I thank those who have read, listened, spoken, or written back. Reading two summers ago in France, at the close of one poem I looked out to see someone in the audience mouth the final words with me. That poem was his as much as it was mine. Something was consumated in that moment. I was elated. I was humbled.

A number of years ago, I heard a story from a colleague about his experience teaching writing to Lakota grade school students in South Dakota. The students were writing poetry. Each session my friend would share with the class some of the fine lines the students had written. The same lines began to reappear in the poetry of the other students. At first he thought plagiarism. Then he began to understand the honor involved and the spirit of community this cross-pollination expressed. For a final project the class constructed a single poem from the many fine lines they had written.

The poem that concludes this book comes from the spirit of that moment in France and from the spirit of that multi-authored Lakota poem, from a seeing into the larger experience of poetry, as collaboration and celebration of influence. It is a poem constructed of the many connections my writing and living has to the stories, experiences, and writings of others. It celebrates the woven story paths of Indian nations by building itself partly from the words of other Native authors.

Y2K Indian

Another absentee Indian
outside White Earth
hand reaches from dream
curves toward paddle
wakes touches absence.
4 *a.m. loneliness*
settles beside me
in a king-size bed
turns up the ticking
on the mantle clock.
Distant dog barks,
may flies crack
against window glass.
I wait for dawn light.

Long nights
sifting memories
sinking spent into morning.
Recall what you said
the old man said
Indian people were not
meant to live in
cities, and none do.
Some reside there
but none live there.

Another absentee Indian
calling myself home.
Do I begin with the songs
whose words I've lost

forgotten
or shoved into drawers
of my past
like so many green stamps?
Or the give-away fabric
small yellow flowers
waiting to be sewn
into garments
for children not yet born?

One finds the way by heart,
you say.
Humbled
I begin
shucking
layers of easy Indian-ness
dig under
at last
uncover
the wound beneath the flesh
that might be all that remains.
It pulses, flutters, throbs with something
I refuse to name.

Remembrance wakens.
I smell the wind for my ancestors.
They have not gone.
I follow the pine scent of their passing
find their images
reflected in the car mirror
the splattered window glass
the bank teller's eye
know they are following me
follow the trickroutes.

They move with me
easily passing
between wilderness and civilization
the university and the pow-wow circuit
the church pew and the cedar smoke circle.

Finding their reflections
harbor mine
I become comfortable
with the story of doubleness
learn *survival this way.*
Another Y2K Indian
writing the circle
of return.